FORTS &
CASTLES

BRIAN WILLIAMS

Viking

Acknowledgments

The publishers would like to thank Jonathan Adams, who illustrated the
see-through pages of this book; James Field, who illustrated the cover;
and the organizations and individuals that have given their permission to
reproduce the following pictures:

American Museum of Natural History/H. Tschopik Jr: 34 top.
Ancient Art and Architecture Collection: 8 top right, 31 top.
AKG, Berlin: 4 top left, 30 top, **/Erich Lessing:** 10 top left, 12 top left, **/Museé Condé, Chantilly:** 26 bottom left.
Bridgeman Art Library/Bibliothèque Nationale, Paris: 22 top. **C.M. Dixon:** 6 top left.
Explorer: 38 top. **Werner Forman Archive/Burke Collection, New York:** 32 bottom.
Sonia Halliday Photographs/F.H.C. Birch: 23 top right, 29 top left, **/Jane Taylor:** 4 bottom left.
Robert Harding Picture Library: 17 top, **/D. Harissiadis © George Rainbird:** 8 top left.
Michael Holford Photographs: 10 top right, 11 bottom left, 20 bottom, 21 top. **Imperial War Museum:** 44 top.
A.F. Kersting: 23 bottom. **Arxiu MAS:** 29 bottom, **/Museo Ejército, Madrid:** 29 top right.
Peter Newark's Military Pictures: 42 top right, 42 top left.
Peter Newark's Western Americana: 40 top left, 40 top right. **James Putnam:** 7 bottom right.
Royal Armouries: 37 top right. **Royal Ontario Museum:** 15 bottom right.
Scala/Bargello, Florence: 39 bottom, **/Museo della Civiltà Romana, Rome:** 16 top left, 18 top,
/Museo Stibbert, Florence: 32 top left, **/Museum of the City of New York:** 43 top,
/Victoria and Albert Museum, London: 37 top left.
Tony Stone Worldwide/Hideo Kurihara: 5 top right. **Zefa Picture Library:** 19 top.

Illustrators
Jonathan Adams: 4-5 (map icons), 6 top, 9, 24-25, 26-27,
27 top and bottom right, 33, 35 bottom right, 38, 41.
James Field (Simon Girling): cover.
Terry Gabbey (Associated Freelance Artists): title page, 7,
8, 10, 14, 15, 16-17, 21, 32, 43.
André Hrydziuszko: 6 bottom, 16 top, 20, 31, 42.
Ron Jobson (Kathy Jakeman): 44, 45.
Nigel Longden: 11, 28, 39, 40.
Kevin Madison: 4-5 (base maps).
Angus McBride (Linden Artists): 12-13, 18-19, 22-23,
30, 34-35, 36, 37, 46-47.

Published by the Penguin Group
Penguin Books USA Inc., 375 Hudson Street, New York, New York 10014, U.S.A.
Penguin Books Ltd, 27 Wrights Lane, London W8 5TZ, England
Penguin Books Australia Ltd, Ringwood, Victoria, Australia
Penguin Books Canada Ltd, 10 Alcorn Avenue, Toronto, Ontario, Canada M4V 3B2
Penguin Books (N.Z.) Ltd, 182–190 Wairau Road, Auckland 10, New Zealand

Penguin Books Ltd, Registered Offices: Harmondsworth, Middlesex, England

First published in Great Britain by Hamlyn Children's Books,
an imprint of Reed Children's Books Limited, 1994
First published in the United States of America by Viking,
a division of Penguin Books USA Inc., 1995

1 3 5 7 9 10 8 6 4 2

Copyright © Reed International Books Limited, 1994

All rights reserved

Library of Congress Catalog Card Number: 94-60536

ISBN 0-670-85898-6

Printed in Belgium

CONTENTS

FORTS AND CASTLES

Soldiers and civilians defend the battlements of a castle in the Middle Ages. For hundreds of years stone castles were the strongholds from which kings and nobles ruled and defended their lands.

Krak des Chevaliers, formidable on a hilltop in Syria. Much of this great fortress was built by Christian Crusader knights, but the square tower in the outer walls was added by Muslim builders.

For thousands of years, forts and castles have played an important part in people's lives. Fortified walls were built not just for defense against enemies, but to dominate the countryside and impress allies. Within castle walls people lived and sheltered. Kings held court in them, and armies strove to capture them.

BEGINNINGS

From the earliest days, people built their homes in places where they felt safe from wild animals and other enemies, such as on a hilltop. They often surrounded their homes with fences of branches or thorny bushes. The first walled towns were built about 10,000 years ago. Many of them had great wealth based on farming, craft, or trade, and they soon became targets for greedy neighbors.

As well as protecting their towns and cities, rulers wanted their own palaces to be well defended. There they would be safe from enemies who broke into the city, or even from their own rebellious subjects. A ruler's defended palace, or citadel, came to dominate many cities.

Fort Sumter

U.S. cavalry forts

Sacsayhuaman

Wherever people fought wars, they built fortifications. There are forts and castles in Africa, America, Asia, Europe, and Oceania. The maps show the location of the main forts and castles described in this book.

CASTLES AND FORTS

In Europe and much of Asia, the fortified homes of rulers developed into castles. There the rulers lived with their families and followers, governing the land around them. Forts, on the other hand, usually contained only soldiers, supplies, and government officials. They guarded frontiers, harbors, river crossings, roads, and other important places.

In this book you will learn about some of the world's most interesting forts and castles. Today, advanced weapons can reduce the strongest walls to rubble in seconds. The age of the castle is over. But when you see pictures of castle ruins or visit them, remember that the stones once echoed to the marching feet of soldiers, the chatter of workmen and servants, and the gossip of traders and travelers.

In the 19th century, fantastic castles like this one in Bavaria, Germany, were built as homes for rich people. Such castles were often made to look like fairy-tale castles, or even partly ruined. They were never intended to be used in war.

Medieval castles

Verdun

Constantinople

Great Wall of China

Vauban forts

Moorish castles

Crusader castles

Golconda

Japanese castles

Motte and bailey castles

Celtic hill forts

Hattusas

Tiryns

Roman forts

Masada

Lachish

Maori forts

HATTUSAS

The influence of the Hittites spread across the Near East. This relief of a Hittite horseman was found in Syria.

The walls and towers of Hattusas were a formidable defense. Inside, the Hittites skillfully built on and around the rocky slopes, using huge blocks of granite and limestone.

More than 3,000 years ago a warrior-people called the Hittites conquered a large empire in what is now Turkey and Iraq. Their kings built a fortified city, a fortress called Hattusas. The ruins of this walled city, with its ruler's palace and temples, are near Boğazköy, a village in Turkey.

A NATURAL FORTRESS

The Hittites found what every fort-builder looked for: a natural stronghold that they could make even stronger. A bleak mountain slope rose high above a flat plain. Two streams flowed close by, ensuring a supply of fresh water. Traders passed through a small village nearby.

On the slope, the builders dug a ditch and raised an earth bank, or rampart, behind it. They built two walls of stone blocks, strengthened by towers and topped with battlements made from mud bricks and wooden beams. The builders also added a tunnel so that soldiers and messengers could leave the city in secret.

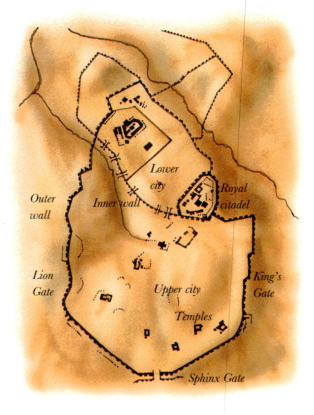

A plan of Hattusas. Long forgotten, the city's ruins were rediscovered in the 19th century.

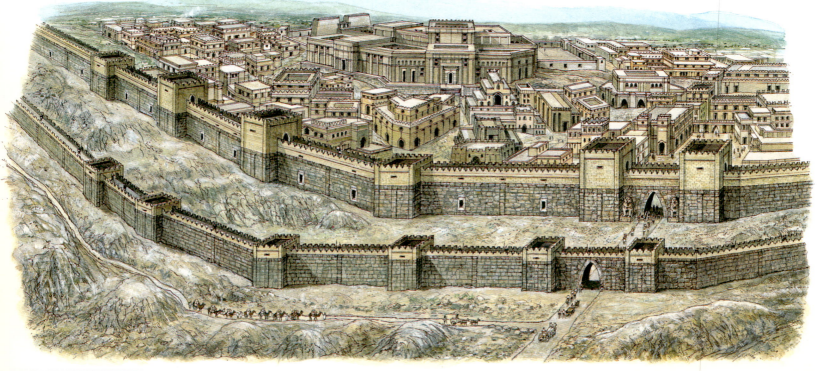

A farmer entering Hattusas has his cartload of grain checked by an official (left). Farmers brought wheat, barley, honey, and vegetables into the city. The bottom picture is based on a relief in an Egyptian temple called the Ramesseum (built in 1280 B.C.). It shows Egyptian soldiers attacking a Hittite fortress while Hittites try to hurl them from the walls.

IMPERIAL CAPITAL

Hattusas, once a windswept trading post, became a powerful city-state and then the imperial capital. From about 1500 B.C. it was the heart of the Hittite empire. Travelers entered the city through one of its arched stone gates. These included the Lion Gate, guarded by stone lions, and the Sphinx Gate. The king had his own gate, the King's Gate. Into the city came farmers with cartloads of food for the city's markets, and merchants with goods loaded on camels and donkeys. Out clattered Hittite soldiers in their three-man chariots.

In the city's streets, foreign ambassadors mingled with traders who journeyed from afar to reach the city of the Hittite kings. Within the walls were several large temples. Inside, surrounded by tall stone columns, were inner rooms or sanctuaries. In these sacred rooms were statues of the gods worshipped by the Hittites.

RISE AND FALL

Hattusas had many private houses, and separate areas for government buildings. From his palace, or citadel, the king could gaze across his city. The citadel was a fortress within a fortress. In its great hall, the king received visitors. He had luxurious royal apartments, and many servants. These included scribes who recorded Hittite triumphs on clay scrolls and stored them in the royal library.

Hittite power lasted until 1100 B.C. Under pressure from migrating tribes, the Hittite empire collapsed and the royal city of Hattusas was destroyed.

TIRYNS

The Mycenaean soldiers wore metal armor made from bronze plates. On their heads they wore leather caps or helmets covered with boars' tusks or studded with metal discs. They fought with swords and spears.

The Mycenaeans were a rich and powerful people who lived in what is now Greece. About 3,500 years ago they built one of the ancient world's greatest fortified palaces, or citadels. It was called Tiryns, and its ruined walls still stand on a hillside in Greece.

THE MYCENAEANS

The Mycenaeans came to Greece from the east, perhaps from the land we now know as Iran. They made tools and weapons of bronze, and they built fortified towns with stone walls and towers for defense.

Tiryns was one of the greatest of their citadels. It was built when the Mycenaeans were facing attacks from foreign enemies. The builders chose their site well, for Tiryns stands on a flat hilltop. An enemy army trying to attack had to climb the hillside before tackling the mighty walls of the fortress itself.

A WORK OF GIANTS

The walls of Tiryns were over 65 feet high and 30 feet thick. They were made of huge blocks of stone. Gigantic stones like this are called "Cyclopean" stones, because the Greeks told stories of how giants called Cyclopes had helped in the building of Tiryns and other great forts.

This picture is based on a wall-painting found at Tiryns. The woman's elegant hairstyle and dress were fashionable on the wealthy island of Crete. Cretan styles in art and dress were copied by the Mycenaeans.

ROYAL SPLENDOR

Tiryns was the home of a powerful king. His palace was a stronghold, meant to awe enemies and friends alike. Visitors marveled, comparing Tiryns with the pyramids of Egypt. The main gate was at the top of a steep ramp, guarded by a high tower. Once inside, people on foot or in chariots could go to the lower citadel or toward the gate of the upper citadel. More passages and gates lay beyond the main gate, before the upper citadel's courtyard and halls were reached.

Soldiers attacking Tiryns had to turn to climb the ramp so that their right side (and sword arm) faced toward the wall and their left side (and shield arm) away from it. This exposed them to arrows and stones from the defenders.

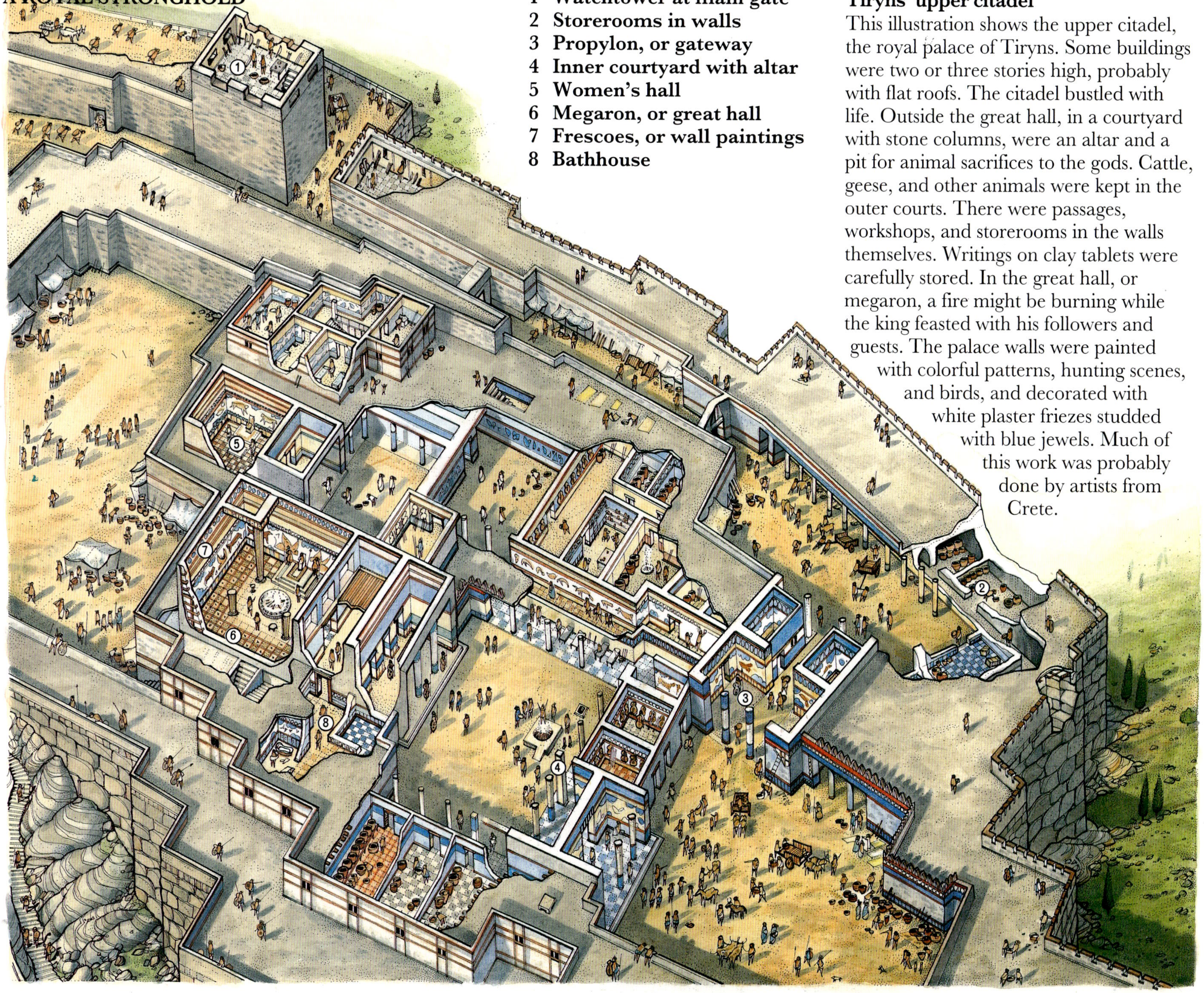

ROYAL STRONGHOLD

Tiryns' upper citadel

This illustration shows the upper citadel, the royal palace of Tiryns. Some buildings were two or three stories high, probably with flat roofs. The citadel bustled with life. Outside the great hall, in a courtyard with stone columns, were an altar and a pit for animal sacrifices to the gods. Cattle, geese, and other animals were kept in the outer courts. There were passages, workshops, and storerooms in the walls themselves. Writings on clay tablets were carefully stored. In the great hall, or megaron, a fire might be burning while the king feasted with his followers and guests. The palace walls were painted with colorful patterns, hunting scenes, and birds, and decorated with white plaster friezes studded with blue jewels. Much of this work was probably done by artists from Crete.

1 Watchtower at main gate
2 Storerooms in walls
3 Propylon, or gateway
4 Inner courtyard with altar
5 Women's hall
6 Megaron, or great hall
7 Frescoes, or wall paintings
8 Bathhouse

THE SIEGE OF LACHISH

"Sennacherib, king of Assyria came up against all the fortified cities of Judah and took them." This is how the Bible describes the devastating campaign when the Assyrians invaded Judah (Palestine). The Assyrians earned a reputation as cruel, bloodthirsty conquerors. At the siege of Lachish in 701 B.C. they showed that no wall—whether made of stone or brick—was safe from their siege machines.

ASSYRIA'S POWER

The Assyrians lived in Mesopotamia (now mostly Iraq). Their empire was at its height from about 900 B.C. to 600 B.C. The warlike Assyrian kings led well-organized armies of armored foot-soldiers, cavalry, horse-drawn chariots, and siege machines.

Sennacherib was one of the most feared of the Assyrian kings—the Hebrew prophet Isaiah described him as an instrument of God's anger against the Hebrews. When King Hezekiah of Judah defied the mighty Sennacherib, his people paid a terrible price.

An Assyrian soldier carries off loot from the defeated city of Lachish. Captured cities were usually stripped of everything the victorious army could carry.

The Assyrian siege machines trundled into battle on wheels. Iron-tipped rams were swung on ropes, and wall-breakers were used to lever and smash loose the stones and bricks.

> **Hezekiah of Judah did not want to put himself under my yoke. I besieged 45 of his 46 towns... I conquered them... I looted the towns and took away as prisoners 200,000 people.**
>
> ——— *Sennacherib* ———

The peoples of the Near East built in brick as well as in stone. The towering ziggurat (pyramid) of Ur in Sumeria, for example, was built largely of bricks in about 2100 B.C. The first brick-makers used river mud mixed with straw, shaped in molds and dried in the sun. Oven-dried bricks were harder, but not even the hardest bricks could withstand Assyrian battering rams.

THE SIEGE OF LACHISH

Lachish, a city in Judah, was just one of the cities that fell to the hammer blows of the Assyrian siege machines. The Assyrians surrounded the city, building earth ramps and using wooden siege towers from which soldiers could attack the battlements. They brought up wheeled battering rams and wall-breakers to pound the walls. As the attack began, some women and children managed to flee the city.

BREACHING THE WALLS

Assyrian archers, sheltered behind basketwork shields, fired at the defenders, who replied with stones and arrows, and flung blazing torches onto the siege towers. The Assyrians inside them threw buckets of water over the towers' leather-covered sides to quench the flames.

Meanwhile, Assyrian miners hacked at the wall with hammers and crowbars, while the massive rams swung and wall-breakers rose and fell like giant axes. As soon as the wall was breached, soldiers stormed into Lachish. As usual, the Assyrians showed no mercy. Those people who were not killed were led away as captives to a life of slavery.

Once inside the walls (right) the Assyrians overwhelmed the defenders. The Assyrians wore armor made of iron. Their swords were also made of iron, and were stronger than the bronze weapons used by most of their foes. Some of the defeated people were impaled on stakes (above), as a lesson to anyone else who might defy the Assyrians.

11

HILL FORTS

The Celts wore iron helmets like this one made in central Europe about 2,500 years ago.

In many parts of the world, forts were not large buildings of rock or stone. Instead, people and their animals sheltered in hilltop villages and forts, protected by fences, walls, and ditches.

FORTIFIED FARMS

The Celts of central and western Europe lived in groups or tribes from about 500 B.C. They were farmers who lived in villages with houses made of wood, stone, or wattle and daub (woven sticks and mud). They were also fierce fighters. Around every village was a fence to protect the villagers and their animals from thieves and raiders. They also added ditches and ramparts as extra defenses.

EARTH WALLS

Many Celts built fortified settlements on hilltops. Celtic fort-builders began by digging a ditch. Some hill forts had two or three ditches ringing the hilltop. The soil they dug out of the ditch was piled up to make a bank, or rampart, above it. More soil was dug out from the hilltop to make the rampart higher. This left a hollow, inside which the people built their houses. On top of the rampart was a wall of earth, clay, chalk, or stones. This wall was topped with a fence of woven sticks or thorns.

In Scotland there are remains of "glass-walled" forts. They were made of stones and timber. When they burned down, the stones melted to a glassy mass.

Some Celtic warriors rode into battle in chariots pulled by horses. The warriors leaped down to fight on foot. The drivers could later collect them and speed them to safety.

SEEKING SHELTER

From the hilltop, farmers could watch over their grazing sheep and cattle. If enemy warriors were spotted, the herdsmen swiftly drove their animals into the fort, where everyone took shelter. Hill forts were not permanent homes for the whole community; people living outside moved into the fort when there was trouble.

When lookouts or patrols spied enemies approaching, the people drove their sheep and cattle into the fort. Everyone took refuge inside as warriors prepared to defend the gateway and ramparts. The hill fort probably protected the food stores of the surrounding area as well as of its own villagers. Hill forts might also have served as religious and trading centers.

MAIDEN CASTLE

The Celts who lived in Britain before the Romans came in A.D. 43 built some very big hill forts. One of the largest is Mai Dun or Maiden Castle in England. Its ramparts and ditches were a daunting obstacle for an enemy army, for earth banks resisted fire and battering rams. The gate was hidden at the end of a maze-like passage between high embankments.

Maiden finally fell to the Roman army. The Romans bombarded the defenders with stone-throwing catapults and giant crossbows before storming the gates.

MAORI FORTS

The Maoris of New Zealand also built hilltop fort-villages, called pas. A stockade of wooden stakes was surrounded by a ditch. Capturing a hill fort was a great prize, for inside were food storehouses. The victors took these as booty. Maories never burned captured forts.

The Maoris of New Zealand built hill forts, too, from about A.D. 900. Maori warriors who boldly stood on the fighting platforms won admiration for their bravery as they hurled insults and weapons. But with no battlements for protection, they were easy targets. Inside the fort, other men poked long spears through slits in the stockade to keep attackers at long range.

THE GREAT WALL OF CHINA

Shih Huang Ti was an all-powerful ruler. His word was law throughout China. Imperial officials kept a nervous watch on progress as the Great Wall grew slowly, stone by stone.

In 214 B.C. the first emperor of all China, Shih Huang Ti, ordered the building of a great wall. Millions of slave-laborers were marched to China's mountain and desert frontiers to build this vast defensive barrier.

A HUGE ENDEAVOR

The wall was the greatest building project ever attempted. The longest wall on Earth, it is still a marvel today. The total length of the wall, with branches, is almost 4,000 miles. On one side of the wall was "civilization": the rich farms and towns of China. Beyond it were the grassy steppes, where only nomads, the wandering people of the plains, roamed.

A GRAND VISION

The wall was the emperor's grand vision, grander than the imperial palace on which 700,000 workers had labored. The wall would defend China from invasion by the "barbarian" nomad hordes.

The emperor sits there by himself and the people of the empire obey him like one body.

— Chinese philosopher —

BUILDING THE WALL

All the work was done by hand. Men dug sand and gravel, broke stone with hammers, carried rubble in baskets, and struggled beneath the weight of heavy road stones. The officials in charge of building the wall were terrified that the emperor would find fault with their work. Any laborer who left too large a gap between stones was executed. Thousands of workers died from disease, injuries, overwork, and hunger.

The wall was built to last. In the mountains, the planners chose their route well, snaking along the crests of rocky ridges. In desert regions an extra outer wall was built to hold back the shifting sand.

Although the Chinese were practical and inventive, they had no machines to do heavy building work. So the Great Wall was built by millions of people using their bare hands. Most of the workers were convicts and prisoners of war, who were considered expendable. They built the outer stone walls then filled them in with rubble.

THE ENEMY WITHOUT

Not all of the wall was new. Some old border walls were rebuilt and joined to new sections. Much of the wall was a simple earth and turf bank. But long sections were made of stones, with watchtowers about 40 feet high every 200 feet: the toiling laborers built 40,000 of them. On these sections was a paved road wide enough for six horses to ride abreast.

Thousands of soldiers were needed to guard the gates and patrol the 30-foot-high wall. They checked travelers and merchants who passed through the gates. Messengers on horseback galloped along the roadway, and signal fires could be lit to send even faster warning of an attack. In some places, soldiers swept smooth stretches of sand outside the wall—so that spies would leave telltale footprints.

NO REAL DEFENSE

The wall reassured China's rulers, but it was difficult to guard every section of such a long wall. When the Mongol leader Genghis Khan invaded China in the 13th century, his horsemen rode in through an open gate.

The Great Wall did not keep out all China's enemies. Nor could it protect the riches in Imperial tombs from grave-robbers. This pottery tower is a model of a tower used to keep watch over the burial grounds of the Han emperors.

15

ROMAN FORTS

The Romans' gold and silver standards were the pride of the army and would be defended fiercely. Each century (about 80, not 100, men) had a standard (above left). The eagle of the legion (above right) was guarded carefully and left camp only when the legion marched into battle. The loss of an eagle in battle was considered a terrible humiliation.

A Roman cavalry fort. In the foreground are the barracks for the soldiers. In the center is the headquarters building with a parade ground, flanked on the left by a storehouse and hospital, and on the right by the commander's quarters and offices. At the back are workshops and stables for the horses.

The Roman army was expert at both fighting and engineering. Roman soldiers built bridges, roads, and forts. From forts large and small they made war and kept the peace across the Roman Empire.

GUARDING THE EMPIRE

The Romans needed large bases for their legions. Each legion had up to 6,000 soldiers, so their base camps were like military towns. Smaller forts (called *castella* in Latin, from which comes our word "castle"), like those along Hadrian's Wall on the northern fringe of Roman Britain, were used to guard the frontiers.

A typical Roman fort was rectangular, with turf or stone walls up to 13 feet high. Inside lived 800 men. There were four gates, one in each wall, and two roads crossing the fort. Within the walls were long buildings used as barracks for the soldiers. They were divided into eight-man rooms. There were also regimental offices, the commander's house, a parade ground, a granary or grain storehouse, a cookhouse, a hospital, stables for horses, storehouses, and workshops.

SOLDIER-BUILDERS

Even when on the march, the soldiers made fortified camps every night. They slept in tents, protected by ditches and fences of sharpened stakes. These same soldiers also built the permanent forts. First surveyors marked out the site, and soldiers with axes and spades cleared the ground, cutting down trees and digging the foundations. Then the carpenters, stonemasons, and plasterers started work on the buildings.

The Romans also used their construction skills when attacking enemy strongholds. They would surround the enemy to prevent them from getting out and rescuers from getting in. Their siege works included trenches and ramparts, moats, and booby traps— covered pits and spikes buried in the ground.

IMPRESSING THE ENEMY

The Romans cleverly made their own forts look stronger than they really were. Most fort buildings had wooden frames covered with wattle and daub. The walls were then plastered so the finished building looked as if it was made of stone. A big fort had catapults and slingshots hidden behind the walls.

HADRIAN'S WALL

In A.D. 122 Emperor Hadrian ordered the building of a wall to divide Roman Britain from the unconquered north (Scotland). Hadrian's Wall was built partly of stone, partly of turf. The wall, over 70 miles long, was no barrier to a determined attack by marauding tribes. It was low and had many gates. But the sixteen stone forts and smaller milecastles, garrisoned by Roman soldiers, were effective frontier posts. Each milecastle had gates at the front and rear and small barracks for the soldiers who lived there.

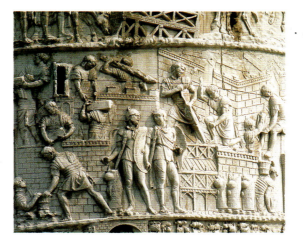

Trajan's Column, a monument in Rome, was dedicated in A.D. 113 in honor of the emperor Trajan's conquest of Dacia. This scene from the column shows Roman soldiers building defenses.

Life on Hadrian's Wall was not very dangerous. There was hardly any fighting. But winters were cold. Soldiers probably appreciated their thick clothing and the warmth of the traveling blacksmith's fire.

MASADA

Roman soldiers were good builders, but they were also skillful at siegecraft, seizing other armies' fortifications. The siege of Masada during the first Jewish revolt against Roman rule is one of the most famous and tragic episodes in the history of warfare.

The armor breastplate, sword, and dagger of a Roman centurion (a middle-ranking officer). In Roman legions, the centurions were the vital link in the chain of command between the general and the soldiers.

Roman soldiers sheltering beneath the testudo or tortoise, a protective shell of shields. In this formation, soldiers could advance under heavy fire. Each man held his shield rim to rim against his comrades' shields to ward off spears and arrows.

HEROD'S STRONGHOLD

Masada (located in present-day Israel) was a hilltop fortress rising more than 1,300 feet above the Dead Sea. On the rocky summit was a flat area. There, in about 35 B.C., King Herod the Great of Judaea built a fortress-palace.

Masada had steep cliffs on all sides. The only way to reach the fortress was up a winding rocky path. The mountain stronghold also had a double wall at the top, with thirty-eight stone towers. At the northern end was the king's palace, an impressive terraced building with towers 100 feet high. To resist a siege, Masada had huge stores, and the armory was stocked with metal and weapons. The storerooms contained enough corn, wine, oil, beans, dates, and other foods to last for years. Water was fed into huge underground tanks from nearby streams.

REVOLT AGAINST THE ROMANS

When Judaea came under the direct control of the Romans, they took over Masada. In A.D. 66 the Jews revolted against Roman rule. A group of Jewish rebels known as the Zealots massacred the Roman garrison and retook Masada.

Rome's vengeance was remorseless. In A.D. 70 the Roman army battered down the walls of Jerusalem and destroyed the Jewish Temple. Soon the Romans turned to Masada. Fifteen thousand men—the Tenth Legion and auxiliaries (foreign support troops)—marched on Masada, bringing siege engines that were dismantled and carried on mules. Against this army, the Jews in Masada numbered 960 men, women, and children.

THE SIEGE

First, the Romans built an encircling wall below the fortress to prevent the Jews from escaping. They set up eight siege camps. Then the soldiers piled up sand and rocks to make an enormous ramp against the cliff. Up this ramp they hauled an iron-clad assault tower. From the tower, slingers and siege engines could fire into the fortress at the defenders. Finally, the stone wall was battered by rams.

The defenders fought heroically. Even when the wall was at last breached by the Romans' incessant attacks, they filled the hole with rubble and timber.

THE END APPROACHES

This won the Jews breathing space, for the battering rams only pounded the makeshift barricade tighter. So the Romans tried a new tactic. They threw blazing torches into the breach, setting fire to the timbers, then withdrew to prepare for the final assault. Fearing they would be made slaves when Masada fell, the Jews chose death instead. The men killed their wives and children, then themselves. When the Romans entered Masada they found only seven women and children left alive, hiding in a pipe. The siege had lasted almost two years.

Masada today (above). The site of the fortress was excavated by archaeologists in the 1960s and remains of the defenses, palace, and storehouses were uncovered. The huge ramp built by the Romans can be seen top right.

The defenders of Masada, outnumbered 15 to 1, could do nothing to halt the Roman assault tower from drawing nearer. As the Roman soldiers attacked the walls, crossbow bolts (thick, blunt arrows) and stones were sent flying into the fortress. The Jews defended the wall grimly, knowing there was no escape.

THE NORMANS

In 1066 William of Normandy crossed the English Channel from France. Quickly overcoming England's defenses, William the Conqueror manacled his new kingdom in a chain of castles.

Heraldry began in Europe during the 1100s. Family emblems helped tell friend from foe in the confusion of battle. This shield of gold lions, one of the first recorded such emblems, was borne by the Earl of Salisbury, son of King Henry II of England.

MOTTE AND BAILEY

The early Norman castles consisted of a great mound of earth, called a motte, with a wooden stockade on top. Inside the stockade was a wooden tower. At the bottom of the mound was a large enclosure called a bailey, often with a ditch or moat around it. The bailey could be reached only by crossing a bridge. Inside the bailey were buildings for the heavily-armored knights and their horses.

A LORD'S STRONGHOLD

The Norman castle was a private fortress, not a refuge for everyone like the old walled towns and hill forts. It was owned by a nobleman or baron who lived in the tower. From his castle, the baron ruled his lands in the king's name and made war on his enemies. Inside the castle, wealthy captives were held until ransoms were paid; less fortunate ones died miserably.

A Norman baron had great power but little comfort. In a hall inside the tower he entertained his followers and guests. There was little furniture: a table, perhaps one high-backed chair for the lord, but benches for the rest. Smoke from an open fire drifted up through a hole in the roof. At night everyone slept on the rush-strewn floor, except the baron and his wife, who retired to their own small private room, the solar. In winter, the castle was cold and drafty. The windows had wooden shutters, because glass was too costly.

The Normans moved fast to defend their foothold on English soil. This picture from the Bayeux Tapestry shows soldiers raising an earth mound for a castle at Hastings, site of the Norman invasion and victory.

A large motte and bailey castle, which has been expanded as its baron has prospered. Some motte and bailey castles grew into large fortified towns. Around the castle was a ditch or a moat filled with water. Most castles had their own wells for drinking water.

CASTLES OF STONE

The wooden buildings of the early motte and bailey castles were inclined to rot. Also, they could too easily be set on fire or knocked down by battering rams and other siege engines. Soon the wooden castles were being replaced by stronger, more permanent stone buildings.

They filled the land full of castles. They oppressed the wretched people by making them work at the castles . . . and filled them with devils and evil men.

— *Anglo-Saxon Chronicle* —

KEEPS AND CURTAINS

The new castles had a square stone tower, or keep, and outer walls supported by towers. These walls, called curtains, were built as high as possible to prevent attackers from climbing over them on ladders. From behind the indented battlements along the tops of the walls, the defenders could shoot their arrows through the open spaces, then move behind cover to reload.

The stone keeps had walls as thick as 13 feet at the base. Some old mottes collapsed under such a great weight. To make attacks on the doorway more difficult, the keep's entrance was often at the top of a flight of steps. As an additional defense, the lower windows narrowed to slits so that attackers could not climb in, but archers could fire out.

Falaise castle in Normandy. William the Conqueror was born in this castle, the home of the dukes of Normandy. The round tower was added to the square Norman keep in the 13th century.

Norman knights feast with their lord, the baron, and his lady. The baron's great wooden dining table was a prized possession; the other tables were folded away when not in use. Tapestries were hung on the walls for decoration and to keep out drafts. Later stone castles had fireplaces built into the outside walls.

21

CRUSADER CASTLES

Terrible deeds were committed by both sides in the Crusades. Severed heads (above), dead animals, and diseased corpses were hurled over castle walls to add to the defenders' discomfort.

Crusaders praying before battle believed that God was on their side. The Muslims were equally certain that theirs was a holy war, and fought more fiercely in the belief that Paradise awaited those killed in battle.

The Crusades were a series of wars fought between Christian and Muslim armies for control of the Holy Land of Palestine. The Christian soldiers, who gathered from many European countries, were known as Crusaders, "soldiers of the cross."

WALLS AND WELLS

The Muslims were expert castle-builders. For example, the citadel at Cairo, Egypt, had walls ten feet thick and its L-shaped gateways were very difficult to attack. Most Eastern castles were round: not as convenient to fit rooms in as square castles, but harder to batter down or collapse by undermining. Their tall towers were ideal lookout posts.

Castles needed huge supplies of food and—vital in a hot, dry land—a reliable supply of water. Water was drawn from deep wells, and rainwater was channeled into enormous underground storage tanks.

CRUSADER CASTLES

The Crusaders founded four Christian kingdoms in the Holy Land. They took over old castles built by the Byzantines (the descendents of the Eastern Roman Empire) and Arabs, and built many new ones. The largest castles had enough supplies to last five years.

Krak des Chevaliers, pictured on page 4, is the best preserved of all the Crusader castles. This mighty fortress was held for the Crusaders from 1142 until 1271 by the Knights Hospitallers, a religious order of knights. At first Krak had just a single courtyard, but later an outer wall and better protection for the entrance were added. Rock walls fell sheer on three sides of the castle; on the fourth was a moat. To reach the gate, attackers had to climb a narrow path exposed to the defenders' fire. Inside was a twisting vaulted passage, barred by four more gates, and finally the massive keep. Krak also had enormous granaries, a well, a windmill, and even an aqueduct.

A siege during the Crusades (left) was often long and exhausting. As siege engines pounded the castle walls, weary soldiers sweated in heavy armor under the blazing sun. The Crusaders eventually also turned against their ally, the Byzantine Empire. In 1204 they seized Constantinople, the Byzantine capital, whose massive walls (above) had been built in the fifth century.

The Saracens built the magnificent castle at Aleppo in Syria in the 13th century. It shows how difficult these sieges were. The citadel stands on a hill, with a bridge leading across to its gate.

SIEGE AND SLAUGHTER

Krak became the most important of the Crusader fortresses. Despite being attacked many times by the Muslims, its magnificent defenses could not be overcome.

The Crusaders, too, conducted many sieges. In 1189 the soldiers of the Third Crusade set out to capture Acre in Syria. They tried to storm the walls from the sea using siege towers mounted on ships, but were driven away by Greek fire. For two years they tried to starve out the defenders and battered the walls with their largest stone-throwing engines, called petrariae. In the end the Muslims had no choice but to surrender.

LOST BY A TRICK

The capture of Acre did not end the Crusades, which lasted for another hundred years. In 1271 Krak was again attacked, this time by the sultan of Egypt. The Muslims fought their way into the outer courtyard but they could get no farther. Then they sent in a forged letter. Believing the letter contained orders from their superiors, the exhausted defenders gave up and opened the gates.

CRUSADING LESSONS

The Crusaders returned to Europe with hard-won experience of siege warfare. Castle builders in Europe took note, and began designing castles with more than one surrounding wall, adding round towers to protect the weak corners of square castle walls, and copying many other features of Eastern fortresses.

SIEGE!

Through holes in the floor of galleries built out from the top of the wall—called machicolations—defenders could fire arrows or drop rocks, scalding water, or boiling oil on the enemy.

Machicolations

Sometimes an army would try to capture an enemy's castle or fortified town. Unless the castle could be seized by surprise, the army would have to conduct a siege. This could last months or even years.

SURRENDER OR STARVE

Siege warfare changed little in the thousand years from the Romans to the Crusades. Two kinds of siege were common. In the first, the army surrounded the castle and tried to force its way in. In the second, the army tried to starve out the defenders.

1 Siege tower
2 Battering ram in siege tower
3 Miners tunneling under wall
4 Stake-filled ditch
5 Soldiers with scaling ladder
6 Battlements

UNDER SIEGE

The siege pictured here might have happened anywhere in Europe or the Middle East during the Middle Ages. The attacking commander usually began by surrounding the castle or town. Ditches, guard towers, and lines of troops prevented food and aid from getting in. His army set up tents and built siege towers. They also assembled artillery—usually ballistas, mangonels, and trebuchets, creaking wooden contraptions that hurled heavy stones or bolts (thick, blunt arrows). Often, the local townsfolk suffered more than the defending soldiers. The attackers cared little if the townsfolk starved, and the defending soldiers retreated inside the town's castle with most of the food.

A siege during the Crusades (left) was often long and exhausting. As siege engines pounded the castle walls, weary soldiers sweated in heavy armor under the blazing sun. The Crusaders eventually also turned against their ally, the Byzantine Empire. In 1204 they seized Constantinople, the Byzantine capital, whose massive walls (above) had been built in the fifth century.

SIEGE AND SLAUGHTER

Krak became the most important of the Crusader fortresses. Despite being attacked many times by the Muslims, its magnificent defenses could not be overcome.

The Crusaders, too, conducted many sieges. In 1189 the soldiers of the Third Crusade set out to capture Acre in Syria. They tried to storm the walls from the sea using siege towers mounted on ships, but were driven away by Greek fire. For two years they tried to starve out the defenders and battered the walls with their largest stone-throwing engines, called petrariae. In the end the Muslims had no choice but to surrender.

LOST BY A TRICK

The capture of Acre did not end the Crusades, which lasted for another hundred years. In 1271 Krak was again attacked, this time by the sultan of Egypt. The Muslims fought their way into the outer courtyard but they could get no farther. Then they sent in a forged letter. Believing the letter contained orders from their superiors, the exhausted defenders gave up and opened the gates.

CRUSADING LESSONS

The Crusaders returned to Europe with hard-won experience of siege warfare. Castle builders in Europe took note, and began designing castles with more than one surrounding wall, adding round towers to protect the weak corners of square castle walls, and copying many other features of Eastern fortresses.

The Saracens built the magnificent castle at Aleppo in Syria in the 13th century. It shows how difficult these sieges were. The citadel stands on a hill, with a bridge leading across to its gate.

SIEGE!

Through holes in the floor of galleries built out from the top of the wall—called machicolations—defenders could fire arrows or drop rocks, scalding water, or boiling oil on the enemy.

Machicolations

Sometimes an army would try to capture an enemy's castle or fortified town. Unless the castle could be seized by surprise, the army would have to conduct a siege. This could last months or even years.

SURRENDER OR STARVE

Siege warfare changed little in the thousand years from the Romans to the Crusades. Two kinds of siege were common. In the first, the army surrounded the castle and tried to force its way in. In the second, the army tried to starve out the defenders.

1 **Siege tower**
2 **Battering ram in siege tower**
3 **Miners tunneling under wall**
4 **Stake-filled ditch**
5 **Soldiers with scaling ladder**
6 **Battlements**

UNDER SIEGE

The siege pictured here might have happened anywhere in Europe or the Middle East during the Middle Ages. The attacking commander usually began by surrounding the castle or town. Ditches, guard towers, and lines of troops prevented food and aid from getting in. His army set up tents and built siege towers. They also assembled artillery—usually ballistas, mangonels, and trebuchets, creaking wooden contraptions that hurled heavy stones or bolts (thick, blunt arrows). Often, the local townsfolk suffered more than the defending soldiers. The attackers cared little if the townsfolk starved, and the defending soldiers retreated inside the town's castle with most of the food.

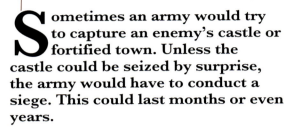

THE DEFENSE

From the walls, the defenders could see most of the enemy's preparations. When attacked, they fired arrows and crossbow bolts from the shelter of the battlements and through narrow slits in the walls. They also fired their own catapults. From wooden shelters jutting out from the walls, they dropped rocks, boiling water, or boiling oil on soldiers below. They pushed away ladders set against the walls. With swords, spears, and clubs they fought off soldiers climbing the tall siege towers. They also tried to set fire to the siege towers.

THE ATTACK

The besiegers crossed the ditch or moat by filling it with rubble and branches. They then rolled siege towers close to the wall, with covering fire from crossbowmen and archers standing behind shelters called mantlets. Soldiers would climb up the towers to get over the walls. At the same time, miners tried to breach the walls, battering holes in them with borers and rams. The ram—an iron-tipped tree trunk on rollers or swung from chains—and its crew were protected by a shelter called a penthouse. Sometimes the attackers dug beneath a wall or tower, making it collapse.

In 1204, at the siege of Chateau Gaillard, the French tried all of these techniques to storm the castle. One line of defenses was even seized by French soldiers who climbed up a toilet drain!

7 Arrow slits
8 Tower flanking the walls
9 Boiling water and rocks being dropped from wooden shelters
10 Ram inside penthouse
11 Soldier crawling up drain

Siege engines included giant crossbows (ballistas), slings drawn back by twisted ropes (mangonels, below), and hinged beams with a weight on one end (trebuchets).

Mangonel

A GOLDEN AGE

Across Europe, castles became centers of government from which kings and barons ruled. Today most castles seem dead and rather dismal, their tumbled walls overgrown with ivy, their echoing halls hung with rusting weapons. Yet once these castles were alive with smells, sounds, and colors.

MEDIEVAL LIFE

Castles in the Middle Ages looked bright and new. Many had whitewashed walls. In the sunlight, with pennants and flags streaming from towers and turrets, a castle was a marvelous sight. All around the castle were fields and meadows tended by peasants and tenant farmers.

This 14th-century French illustration shows that a castle was the center of life in the countryside. The building dominates the landscape and the people who work in it. Only a cathedral could match such size and majesty.

THE GREAT AGE OF CASTLES

By the 13th century, castle life was becoming a little more comfortable. Bathrooms were built into corner towers and outer walls. Rooms were hung with tapestries or painted in bright colors. Soaring roof beams were carved in delicate patterns. In the lord's hall, there were jugglers and jesters, music and dancing, and much feasting.

The square castle with drum-like towers, such as those at Angers in France, was a popular design, but many other shapes were tried, including eight-sided castles. Castle-builders copied ideas from one another. Castles in Spain were decorated in North African Moorish style. In Italy, nobles built towers that rose high above the rooftops of the towns, like medieval skyscrapers.

The keep was the baron's headquarters and stronghold. Building a castle took a great deal of time, effort, and money. Workmen had to be paid for years of labor. Hundreds of cartloads of stone and timber were needed.

great hall

servants' quarters and kitchens

entrance

DEFENSE IN RINGS

Castles became more and more difficult to attack. The concentric, or ring, castle of the 13th century was the pinnacle of medieval castle design. The Crusaders fighting in the East saw Muslim and Greek castles with not just one wall, but two or three rings of walls. Each wall was protected by strong towers, and each was a separate line of defense. The inner walls were highest, so their defenders could fire over the heads of soldiers on the outer walls. Returning Crusaders built similar castles in Europe.

bastion towers *keep* *outer curtain wall* *moat* *barbican*

A typical concentric or ring castle. The outer curtain wall has low bastion towers. There are high towers on the inner wall, a massive gatehouse, and an outer barbican to protect the moat bridge. Soldiers guarded the wall walks and could move from tower to tower through passages in the walls.

BARRING THE GATE

Castle-builders devised many unpleasant surprises for an attacking enemy. They built battlements out from the wall top, so that defenders could drop stones, boiling water, or boiling oil through "murder holes" or machicolations in the overhang.

The gate was shielded by a massive gatehouse. The only way to get to the gate was by crossing a drawbridge, held shut by heavy weights. Beyond that was a portcullis, an iron grille that could be lowered to bar the gateway, and often an outer gatehouse, called a barbican, to protect the moat and drawbridge.

MASTER BUILDERS

Old castles and city walls were often rebuilt, and great kings wanted even greater castles. Edward I, who ruled England from 1272 to 1307, demanded castles to subdue newly conquered Wales. He summoned Master James of St. George, a castle-builder famed throughout Europe, to build them. Master James gathered expert engineers and builders. Aided by hundreds of quarrymen, laborers, metalsmiths, masons, and carpenters, he built for Edward the finest castles of the age.

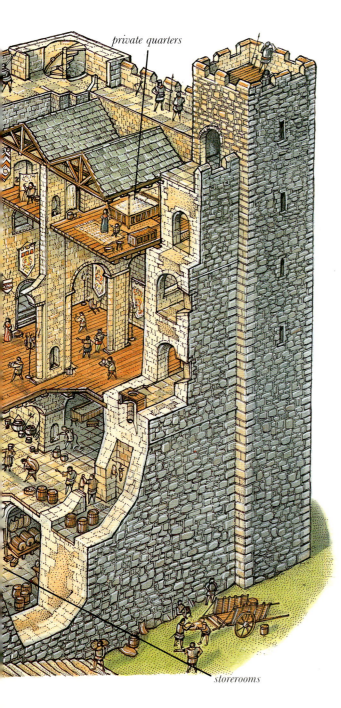

private quarters

storerooms

winding mechanism

drawbridge

counter-weight

moat

This drawbridge could be easily raised or lowered by winding chains inside the gatehouse. It also has a large counterweight at the rear—if the chains are cut by attackers, the counterweight will hold it shut.

THE MOORS IN SPAIN

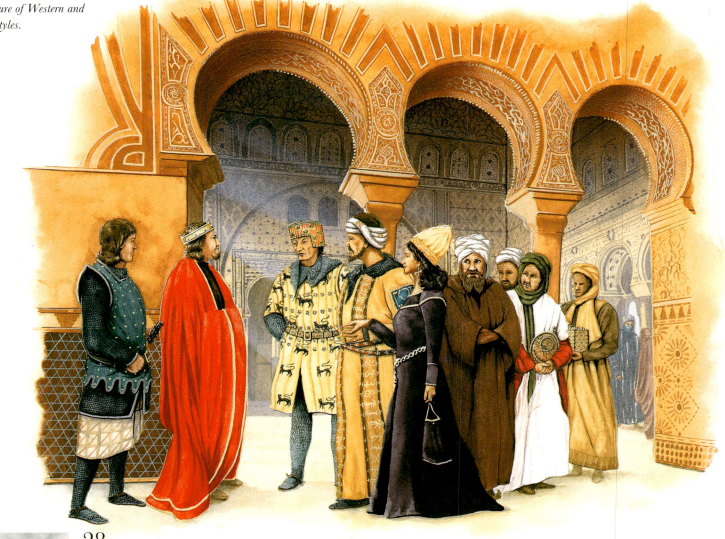

In the eighth century, Muslim Arab invaders from North Africa conquered most of Christian Spain. The conquerors were known as the Moors. They brought new forms of learning and art to Spain, as well as dramatic new castles, called alcazars.

MUSLIM SPAIN

After the Muslim Moors conquered Spain, only the far north of the country had Christian rulers. But in the Moorish kingdoms Christians and Muslims lived together peacefully most of the time. As a result of the conquest, Islamic art and architecture became part of Spanish life.

MOORISH CASTLES

Of course, the Moors still needed to defend themselves against attack, and so they built fortified palaces called alcazars. Alcazar is an Arabic word meaning "fortress" or "fortified palace."

Spain was filled with such castles. Many of the fortresses were built on hills whose steep slopes were a daunting first line of defense. Some were constructed on the sites of old Roman or Visigothic castles. The city of Córdoba—famous for its learning and scholarship—had two alcazars: an older Moorish castle and a later one built by a Christian king. Toledo had five of them!

Moorish visitors to the court of Castile are received by King Alfonso X, who made the alcazar of Segovia his palace in the 13th century. Moorish visitors felt at home in the alcazar because it was decorated in a mixture of Western and Eastern styles.

The alcazar of Segovia stands high above the city, on a narrow rocky plateau. The pointed roofs date from rebuilding by Philip II in the 16th century. In 1862, much of the castle was destroyed by fire. Careful restoration has recreated much of its former splendor.

MOORISH STYLE

The alcazars were splendid buildings, full of rich decoration, such as mosaics (tiled patterns) and wall paintings, in Muslim style. European castles were seldom highly ornamented, inside or out, but the Arabs delighted in geometric patterns. Within the walls of his fortress-palace, a Moorish ruler could enjoy his fountains and gardens, cool pavilions and shaded walks.

SEGOVIA'S ALCAZAR

Many surviving castles can be found in the Segovia region of Castile. The alcazar at Segovia was a great fortress-palace used by the Christian kings of Castile, who had captured the city from the Moors in 1079. As well as building the alcazar, the Castilians reinforced the old Roman walls of the city with over 80 towers.

Although built for Christian kings, the alcazar was a mixture of Christian and Moorish styles. By the 13th century, Segovia had become a center of learning. There, Alfonso X, known as "the Wise," promoted the learning of the Castilian language, which later became Spanish. The alcazar's magnificently decorated Ambassador's Salon was used to host receptions for both rulers and scholars.

THE ARCHBISHOP'S CASTLE

Spanish castle-builders used both stone and brick. Real fortifications tended to have massive stone walls. The powerful fortress of Coca (pictured at the top of the opposite page) was built in the 15th century for the archbishop of Seville. Despite being home to a Christian, Coca was built by Spanish-speaking Muslims, who were considered the best engineers and workers. The brick walls and battlements are decorated in Arab style.

Although imposing, Coca was really a palace rather than a proper fortress, and it might not have lasted long under heavy bombardment. However, it does have a very nasty dungeon for prisoners, a round cell entered through its roof, where every sound echoes chillingly.

THE END OF MOORISH RULE

The Moors governed Spain virtually unchallenged until the 11th century, when squabbles between rival rulers weakened their grip. The country was split into small kingdoms and city-states. The northern Christian kingdoms grew stronger and fought the Moors, gradually recovering more territory. The reconquest of Spain was led by the Castilian kings and Ruy Díaz, "El Cid." By the end of the 13th century only Granada in the south was still ruled by the Moors. It finally fell to the Christian kingdoms in 1492.

This sword belonged to Boabdil, the last Moorish king of Granada, the last of the Moorish kingdoms in Spain. The relief below shows the siege of Granada in 1491. The site from which Boabdil last saw his beautiful city is named El último sospiro del Moro, "the last sigh of the Moors."

THE RENAISSANCE

The Renaissance of the 15th century was a period of upheaval and new ideas in Europe. In warfare, crossbows and catapults gave way to the arquebus (an early musket) and the cannon. The castle-builders now had to meet the challenge of gunpowder.

THE FIRST CANNONS
A picture dated 1326 shows a squat bottle-shaped cannon, one of the first in Europe. Cannons were loaded, or charged, with gunpowder, and fired rounded stones or metal balls. They were clumsy, slow-firing, and unreliable. Often they blew up their own gunners!

Early siege guns (below) were hauled into position and set up on wooden supports in front of the target. These iron cannons fired iron balls or stones rounded to fit into the gun barrel. At the siege of Constantinople in 1453 (right), the Turkish guns managed only seven shots each a day. But they were invaluable in defeating the Byzantine forces. The Byzantine Empire, which had resisted the Muslims and Ottoman Turks for hundreds of years, fell at last.

THE FALL OF CONSTANTINOPLE

The high, relatively thin walls of medieval castles offered poor defense against cannons. In 1453 the Turks captured Constantinople. Their cannons kept up a slow-firing but ceaseless bombardment of the walls until the ancient stonework crumbled. The fall of Constantinople shocked rulers across Europe. The Turks actually captured the city by a commando-style raid through an underground passage, but the cannons' loud message had been clear to all.

Kings and nobles still wanted palaces and country houses. These fine buildings could be made to look like castles, but they could not be defended against guns. Real fortification had to become more scientific. New ideas were needed, and most came from Italy, birthplace of the Renaissance. In an age of frequent wars, artists of genius—such as Dürer, Michelangelo, and Leonardo da Vinci—had new ideas about military engineering as well as sculpture and painting.

Behold the ordnance [cannons] on their carriages, with fatal mouths gaping!

Shakespeare, Henry V

GUNS AND GUNNERS

Soldiers needed forts with strong walls to protect them from cannon-fire, and from which they could fire their own cannons at the enemy. In the 16th century a new type of fort was built along coasts, usually to keep enemy ships away and to defend towns from invasion. Its outer wall was low, rounded, and sloped so that cannon balls would bounce off it. Behind the wall was a broad ledge for standing cannons on. In front of the wall was a ditch and an open space where the approaching enemy could be seen and shot at.

Many of the forts of this new age did not have large garrisons of soldiers. They were made for guns and gunners. The new forts had squat turrets, not high towers. Some had defensive positions, or bastions, sticking out from the walls. From the bastions, the defenders could fire back along the walls with a deadly crossfire.

An early cannon, from a 14th-century manuscript. Although light enough to be handled by one man, this "firestick" was not very accurate or reliable. The gunner rested the gun on a prop, took aim, fired the gunpowder charge—and hoped for the best.

Deal Castle was built in less than two years (1539-40) to defend the English coast. It looks like a flower, with six bastions around the keep. With luck, the castle's gunners could hit ships up to three miles away. In the fort's gunpowder storehouse, or magazine, candle lanterns were set behind glass windows to lessen the risk of accidental explosions.

31

JAPANESE CASTLES

I n the 1500s, Japan was still a medieval society. The emperor ruled in name, but real power lay with the warlords, or daimyos. The warlords led the samurai knights into battle and built castles —bigger than those of Europe and in some ways very different.

AN AGE OF CASTLES

Early Japanese castles were simple wooden towers. Then, in 1576, the powerful warlord Oda Nobunaga built a new castle-palace at Azuchi. It had a seven-story high tower or keep, called a tenshu, surrounded by moats and stone walls. Japan's great soldier-rulers Toyotomi Hideyoshi and Tokugawa Ieyasu followed this lead. They ordered nobles to supply materials and workmen for castles. Sixty thousand men worked on the fortress at Osaka, built in 1578.

Japanese castles had wood-frame walls filled with bamboo and clay, which were then plastered over. Soldiers inside fired muskets and bows though windows closed by wooden shutters. Sieges were rare. Japanese cannons were poor, and, anyway, the samurai soldiers preferred fighting their battles in the open.

Samurai warriors fought for their warlords. They wore armor and their favourite weapon was a curved sword, or katama. However, samurai armor was little protection against a musket fired at close range.

Beyond iron-plated wooden doors were elegant rooms smelling of cedarwood, charcoal grills, and oil lamps. Carpenters, furniture-makers, and painters were employed to decorate the castle's living quarters. Lords lived with their officials and families in a style much admired by foreign visitors.

A MAZE OF CORRIDORS

The tenshu was connected to smaller towers by corridors. The maze of corridors, gateways, and courtyards made it hard for enemy soldiers to penetrate deep into the defenses.

In 1615 Tokugawa Ieyasu, victorious after bloody civil wars, forbade castle-building. He declared, "High walls and deep ditches are the cause of great upheavals when they belong to others." Japan's brief "golden age" of castles was over.

Nijo Castle in Kyoto was built in 1603, when Kyoto was Japan's imperial capital and the home of Tokugawa Ieyasu. This screen painting shows a member of the Tokugawa family driving out of the castle gate in a carriage.

A WARLORD'S STRONGHOLD

Soaring roofs on granite base

The keep, or tenshu, of a Japanese castle such as Himeji, the White Heron castle, stood on a massive stone base. The building on top looked light and delicate by comparison. It had as many as seven floors. Carved figures of dolphins and other creatures decorated the eaves of the tiled roofs. Because earthquakes are common in Japan, the keep was not attached to the stonework, and was flexible enough to absorb the vibrations by "bouncing" rather than collapsing if there was an earthquake.

1 Generals with emperor
2 Tiled roofs
3 Kitchen
4 Shuttered windows
5 Granite stones of base
6 Plaster-covered timber wall
7 Beaters for putting out fires
8 Corridors to small towers
9 Overhangs from which to drop rocks on enemy
10 Soldiers' sleeping area

Stone-dropping chute

SACSAYHUAMAN

Incan tools and weapons were made from stone. Shown here are a tumi, or knife (left), a mace head, and a chisel. The Incas were awed by the Europeans, who had guns and horses, both unknown in South America. Very few Incan objects survive because the Spaniards looted the empire of its treasures, melting down its gold and silver.

The Incas ruled a huge empire of over two million people in ancient South America. In the mountains of the Andes they built stone fortresses that rivaled those of medieval Europe and Asia. Yet in a few years, the Incan Empire was swept away by a handful of invading soldiers from the Spanish Empire, the conquistadores, or conquerors.

A ROYAL FORTRESS

In about 1520 the Incan ruler Pachacuti built a huge fortress overlooking the royal capital of Cuzco. Called Sacsayhuaman, its ramparts zigzagged across the hillside. People marveled, for the walls were made of gigantic stone blocks, some weighing over 100 tons.

AMAZING STONEWORK

A Spaniard later wrote that the stones at Sacsayhuaman were "as big as the trunks of trees of the forest." The Incas did not use mortar to hold together the stones; instead, each block was shaped and positioned with such accuracy that the buildings seemed to be the work of magicians. Inside the walls were three towers, storehouses, and rooms for the garrison. The largest tower contained the ruler's apartments.

Although the Incas did not have artillery, a Spanish soldier declared that the massive walls were too strong to batter down or undermine. Many warriors, however, would be needed to defend the fortress—if anyone dared to attack the mighty Incas.

The Spaniards, led by Pizarro, enter Sacsayhuaman. Twenty thousand workers labored for 60 years to build the fortress. Its walls were likened to the jaws of a puma, the symbol of the Incas' power. The Spanish admired the great stone walls, but were more interested in the Incas' gold and silver.

SPANISH CONQUEST

In 1533 Spanish conquistadores attacked Cuzco. There were only 130 of them, but they were helped by local people who turned against their Incan masters. The Incan ruler had been killed, and Incan weapons were no match for Spanish guns and horses. The Incas retreated and the Spaniards rode into the city and the fortress without a shot being fired.

In 1536 the Incas revolted, seizing back Sacsayhuaman. The Spaniards from Cuzco then recaptured the fortress, but the Incas besieged it for ten more months. They fought off three Spanish rescue expeditions; then a fourth Spanish force relieved the city in April 1537. Today just remnants of Sacsayhuaman's walls survive, because the Spaniards who settled in Cuzco tore down most of the stones to build houses.

Beneath the fortress of Sacsayhuaman was a maze of tunnels twisting and turning underground. By the light of burning torches, soldiers could pass from one tower to another through these secret passages.

A plan of the fortress of Sacsayhuaman, showing the terraced walls and the main buildings.

35

GOLCONDA

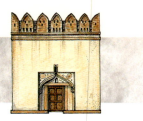

When much of India came under the rule of the Moguls in the 1500s, castle warfare increased. Local rulers built fortresses as symbols of their power, and usually decorated them more richly than European castles.

DIAMOND RICH

One of the greatest Indian fortresses was Golconda in the state of Andhra Pradesh. The city of Golconda became famous in medieval times for its diamonds, which were mined nearby. Its wealthy rulers could afford to build impressive defenses to protect themselves and their riches.

A WALLED CITADEL

Golconda was typical of the hilltop fortresses built all over India. It had thick walls and towers, like castles in Europe and the Middle East, but higher gates—to allow elephants to pass through.

The fortress was built on a hill strewn with granite boulders. It was enclosed by three walls. The outer wall, strengthened by defensive bastions and surrounded by a ditch, protected the city. Eight tall gateways were defended by barbicans and overhanging parapets. Every gate was shielded by a twisting, walled approach, making it difficult for enemy troops to mount a rush attack.

Indian armies used war elephants. As a result, castles were fitted with elephant-proof doors. Rows of iron spikes in the doors stopped the elephants from battering them down with their heads.

FIRE AND FLOOD

During the siege, both sides used guns and explosives. Golconda, like other forts and castles, had been improved so that defenders could fire cannons and muskets from the walls. The besieging Mogul army lost some of its guns when heavy rains flooded their encampment. Later, Golconda's defenders made a surprise attack from the gates, and took a number of captives. The prisoners were fed well (to show that the city had plenty of food) and sent back, with an offer to surrender on fair terms. The emperor refused.

MINES AND COUNTERMINES

The Mogul soldiers were now suffering from sickness. Their morale slumped further when three attempts to blow up the walls failed miserably—twice the gunpowder packed into tunnels blew up only hundreds of their own men. A third attempt, watched by the emperor himself, fizzled out. Miners from the fort had dug into the tunnel from the other side and removed the powder kegs!

The siege of Golconda ended after eight months. One of the city's officers was bribed to leave a gate unguarded, and Mogul soldiers slipped secretly inside. Not even the strongest walls were proof against treachery.

A mail-and-plate coat worn by an Indian soldier during the 17th century. The metal breastplate gave extra protection against musket fire.

The Moguls tried to scale the walls under cover of darkness, but were foiled by a barking dog. The defenders hurled the emperor's soldiers from their ladders and drove them off with hand grenades.

A siege in Mogul India. Many men and animals were needed to move the heavy cannons into position. The gunners (top) are sheltering from enemy musket fire.

Higher up the hill, a double wall enclosed the citadel. The final defense, at the heart of the fortress, was an inner wall made by joining stonework and rocky outcrops. Some walls were 30 feet thick.

SAVED BY A DOG

Golconda was the capital of an independent Muslim kingdom, one of several in southern India. Within such a fortress, its sultan felt safe. But in 1687 the great Mogul emperor Aurangzeb, who ruled from Delhi, sought to add Golconda to his own Muslim empire. His army attacked the city, but the defenders resisted stoutly. After four months, a small band of Mogul soldiers succeeded in climbing the walls by night. A barking dog roused the guards and the raiders were driven back into the ditch. The sultan of Golconda honored the dog with a gold collar.

VAUBAN FORTRESSES

Marshal Sébastien le Prestre de Vauban (1633-1707) was France's leading military engineer. France was Europe's strongest power, and Vauban had the men and money to plan and build as he wished. France was eventually defeated by the combined forces of Britain, the Netherlands, and the Austrian Empire.

This side view of a Vauban fort's wall (below) shows the firing positions of the soldiers and cannons. The star shape (right), with bastions giving all-around visibility for gunners, was used for forts and town defenses.

By the 17th century, military engineers were as important as generals in winning wars and deciding who ruled nations. Warfare was becoming more technical, and fort-builders developed increasingly sophisticated defenses.

FIGHTING BY RULES

In the 17th and 18th centuries most kings left the business of war to professional soldiers and engineers. Although cannons were now mounted on wheels, armies marched slowly into battle, dragging their guns and supply wagons behind them. Towns guarding main roads, river crossings, and harbors were fortified to block enemy advances. Battles were fought according to rules and traditions.

THE MASTER PLANNER

By the second half of the 17th century, under Louis XIV, France was Europe's strongest nation, and it fought many wars against its neighbors. France's best military engineer was Sébastien le Prestre de Vauban. In 1655 Louis made Vauban his chief engineer. His talents soon came to the fore during sieges in the Low Countries (modern Belgium and Holland).

Vauban rose to be a Marshal of France, his country's highest military rank. His ideas were used in building or rebuilding 160 fortresses and towns. The hard-working Vauban personally directed over 40 sieges, all of them successful.

Never do uncovered and by force what can be done by industry... The art of fortifying does not consist in rules and systems, but solely in good sense and experience.

— *Vauban* —

TRENCH WARFARE

Vauban believed soldiers should use common sense, not follow rules blindly. He was a patient planner, of attack as well as of defense. If soldiers besieging a fortress charged across open ground, many would be shot down. He decided it was better to dig a series of "sap and parallel" trenches. Moving forward from their own lines, Vauban's men dug trenches or "saps" first forward toward the enemy, then sideways (parallel to the fort's wall), then forward again. In this way, hidden from the enemy guns in the maze of trenches, they could get near enough to storm the wall.

The cannons of Vauban's time were not much better than those used in the previous century. They were not very accurate, and fired solid balls, which often bounced harmlessly off a fort's glacis, or sloping wall. So Vauban grouped his cannons in batteries, to concentrate fire at weak spots.

glacis

firing position

cannon

bridge

covered walkway

star shape (allows defensive crossfire along walls)

citadel (in fort) or town (in fortified town)

ravelin

ditch

bastion

glacis (slope)

THE SCIENCE OF WAR

Fort-builders used mathematics to work out the best angles of attack and lines of fire. Many of the forts built by Vauban and his followers were star-shaped. This shape gave defenders good all-around views and lines of fire. Soldiers rushed along covered walkways to their firing positions. Cannons fired over the wall or through gaps in it. By the end of the 18th century, a single tower in a fort might have nearly 30 guns.

Bastions shaped like arrowheads stuck out from the outer wall. Gunners inside had a clear view to both front and side of enemy troops. From ravelins and redoubts (islandlike mini-forts within the main fort), the defenders pinned down the attackers with crossfire. If the enemy broke through the outer defenses, troops in the mini-forts could hold out while their comrades withdrew through tunnels or across moat bridges into the central citadel.

COLONIAL WARS

European nations also built Vauban forts in their colonies in Africa, Asia, and North America. Some were as strong as any in Europe, too strong to be captured easily. So daring commanders chose "impossible" alternatives. In 1759 the British army attacked the French at Quebec in Canada. The city walls were too formidable to attack directly, so General Wolfe led his soldiers up "unclimbable" cliffs and took the fort by surprise. But the British were not always so successful. When facing revolution in their American colonies, their soldiers were often isolated in the forts, leaving the Americans in control of the countryside.

Sappers digging a trench outside a fortified town. They are using gabions (baskets filled with earth) as movable shields against musket bullets. The grenadier on the left is hurling a smoking grenade, probably into an enemy countertrench.

Cannons changed little from the 1500s to the 1700s, and many were ornately decorated. From the mid-1700s armies had cannons that fired more accurately over longer distances.

39

A CAVALRY FORT

The cavalry forts of Hollywood films and legend really did exist. But real fort life was tough. Soldiers and their families shared the hardships of frontier life, with few comforts.

STOCKADES AND SETTLERS

The first European settlers in North America built wooden stockades for protection against wild animals and the sometimes hostile Native Americans. Later, in the 18th century, the French and British in Canada and the Spanish in Florida built army forts much like those in Europe.

As the independent United States grew, settlers moved steadily westward. By the 1840s, wagon trains were heading west across the Great Plains and the Rocky Mountains. The invading settlers were resisted by the Native Americans, who fought to defend their lands and hunting grounds.

A Native American war club. Native American warriors used both traditional weapons and rifles, but were no match for the U.S. Army, which was equipped with repeating rifles and cannons, and backed by industrial technology.

An army revolver. The guns of the U.S. cavalry had a rate of fire and power unmatched by any Native American weapons.

POLICING THE FRONTIER

The United States government sent the army to protect the settlers. After the Civil War of 1861-65, the U.S. Army had only 25,000 men, so frontier cavalrymen had to patrol vast areas of wilderness. The fort commander represented the federal government in distant Washington; he and his soldiers had to carry out many duties. A fort usually had the only doctor and hospital for many miles.

LONELY OUTPOSTS

The frontier fort was a lonely outpost. It was supplied by wagon trains and riverboats, and later by railroads. Sometimes the fort buildings were grouped inside a wooden stockade. In the desert, where timber was scarce, forts were made of sun-dried mud brick, called adobe.

Native Americans seldom attacked a fort. They had little experience in attacking large fortifications, and had no cannons. They mostly fought in small groups, raiding wagon trains or ambushing cavalry patrols. Big battles were rare. By 1900 the territory wars were over and the story of the frontier fort was at an end.

Sometimes the U.S. cavalry escorted wagon trains carrying settlers. The troopers were armed with rifles and sabers (swords). At night, the wagons were drawn up in a circle as a defense against surprise attacks.

A CAVALRY FORT IN THE 1870s

Everyday life in the fort

In the fort, the soldiers lived and slept in bunks in the barrack rooms. In the mess, or canteen, the cooks served stews made from dried or salted beef, with beans and bread. The diet was supplemented by wild game (deer, jackrabbit, fish), and by vegetables grown by the soldiers' wives in small gardens. The troops could also buy a few luxuries, such as tobacco and alcohol, at the fort's store. When not patrolling, the soldiers drilled on the parade ground in front of the U.S. flag. In some forts the gunpowder was stored underground, even in the middle of the parade ground.

1 Fort commander's HQ
2 Officers' quarters
3 Guard house
4 Hospital
5 Laundry
6 Quartermaster's stores
7 Stables
8 Troopers' barracks
9 Troopers' mess
10 Armory
11 Workshops
12 Fort offices
13 Powder magazine
14 Visiting workers' tents

SIEGE OF FORT SUMTER

Major Anderson of the U.S. Army commanded Fort Sumter. Before the war he had taught gunnery to General Beauregard, now his Confederate enemy.

Inside Fort Sumter during the brief battle in 1861. Amazingly there was no loss of life as the fort's brick walls withstood a tremendous barrage. The defenders, who dug some of their cannons into the fort's courtyard, returned fire, but to little effect.

By the second half of the 19th century, increased firepower and the newly built railroads were changing the way wars were fought. It was now easier to bring overwhelming force against a fortification. But forts remained important as bases for soldiers and for defending towns and ports.

A HARBOR FORT

In December 1860, South Carolina became the first Southern state to break away from the United States. War was near. At this time, Fort Sumter was still being built on an artificial island in Charleston harbor, South Carolina. Manning its uncompleted defenses were just 68 Union (Northern) soldiers led by Major Robert Anderson. Faced by overwhelming odds, the tiny Union garrison in Charleston withdrew to Fort Sumter. There they were surrounded—by water, by 6,000 eager Confederate (Southern) troops, and by artillery. Inside the fort, the men cleaned old cannons so they could be used, increasing their firepower from 15 to 60 guns. Then they could only wait.

A contemporary illustration of the recapture of Fort Sumter in 1865. The actual return was a more formal ceremony.

UNDER SIEGE

Unlike a medieval castle, Fort Sumter was ill-equipped to withstand a long siege. It was designed to defend Charleston harbor from naval attack, not to quell a rebellion. On April 7, 1861, Charleston's traders stopped sending food to the fort. Four days later, Major Anderson refused a Confederate demand to surrender.

THE FIRST SHOT

Finally, at 4:30 a.m. on April 12, the Confederate guns opened fire. It was a historic moment: the beginning of the Civil War. The citizens of Charleston listened to the booming of the cannons and watched from their rooftops as the shells burst around the fort. In the next 34 hours, the Confederate guns fired over 3,300 shells into Fort Sumter. Yet, remarkably, only a horse was killed. The fort's gunners fired back in defiance. Without reinforcements by sea, they had no hope of winning.

THE SURRENDER

Under these impossible conditions, Major Anderson requested a truce. The guns of both sides fell silent, after Fort Sumter's cannons fired a final salute to the Union flag. Tragically, two men were killed accidentally during the ceremony, the only casualties on either side. The garrison were allowed to leave the burning fort, taking the shell-tattered Union flag with them.

In Confederate hands, the repaired and reinforced Fort Sumter proved a tough nut to crack. Union ships attacked the fort several times, but the South held it until February 1865, when Union armies overran South Carolina. On April 14, 1865, Major Anderson was back inside the fort he had defended to hoist the Union flag, the same flag he had borne away four years before. That same night President Lincoln went to a Washington theater— and was killed by an assassin's bullet.

The Confederate bombardment of Fort Sumter was a spectacular sight. The people of Charleston watched the shellbursts with a mixture of excitement and foreboding. Most knew that the attack marked a turning point in the history of the South and of the United States of America. The eventual capture of the fort was a symbolic triumph for the South; the fight for Sumter inspired the defenders of many other forts.

Confederate gunners fight off a Union attack on Fort Sumter in 1863. An island gun-fort like Sumter was difficult to capture, unless its garrison was starved out or attacked by a large fleet and thousands of troops.

THE END OF AN AGE

Soldiers wore metal helmets for protection against flying shrapnel (shell fragments) and bullets. Some wore body armor made from fiber and metal but it was too heavy to be of much use.

By the 19th century, the strongest countries had industries that could supply armies with mass-produced weapons. In 1870-71 the German army used its new firepower to win the Franco-Prussian War against France.

NEW FORTS

In this war, soldiers in the open were cut down by rifles, machine guns, and artillery firing exploding shells. Learning the lessons of the war, France and Belgium built lines of huge concrete forts to defend their land frontiers. These forts were mostly buried underground to make them more difficult targets. The living quarters and magazines were all beneath the ground. Only the steel gun turrets, called cupolas, were slightly exposed. The forts were protected by layers of concrete, with sand in between to absorb the force of exploding shells. These forts played a major part in World War I.

WORLD WAR I

At first neither side could break through the other's defenses. Exhausted, troops dug into defensive trenches stretching hundreds of miles. When generals ordered advances, millions of men died in useless attacks across muddy wastelands of shell holes and barbed wire. Often they never even reached the enemy lines. At Verdun in France, where mighty forts defended important factories and railways, the German army gathered 1,200 guns. These fired two million shells in the first two days of a massive eight-month battle in 1916. Despite the loss of some key forts, the French army held Verdun—but at a cost of over 300,000 dead on each side.

During the war, aircraft were used for the first time to drop bombs on enemy defenses. Then the tank was invented. This steel machine could crawl through the mud and over the trenches, and break through barbed wire.

A World War I fort in Belgium. It had guns mounted in steel turrets buried in concrete and brick. Most of the fort was hidden deep underground, protected from enemy artillery fire. The soldiers lived and worked underground, keeping in touch with other forts by radio.

THE LAST GREAT FORTS

Trenches and concrete forts were little
defense against these new weapons, which
could break through or bypass them.
Nevertheless, in the 1930s the French
government built the Maginot Line to
deter another German attack. Consisting
of 58 large forts and almost 400 smaller
blockhouses, the defenses included
artillery, machine guns, ditches, and iron
rails driven into the ground to halt tanks.
However, in 1940 the German armies
invaded Belgium, then advanced into France
through its less heavily defended northern
frontier, which the Maginot Line did not
protect. When finally attacked, the French
soldiers in the forts fought well. But the
Maginot Line had not saved the country.

No system of forts can resist the mobility
and destructive power of modern tanks,
planes, and guided missiles. That is why the
Maginot Line failed. Today its massive
concrete and steel forts are half-forgotten.

KEY DATES AND GLOSSARY

This book can describe only a selection of the forts and castles built throughout the world in the last 10,000 years. A more complete chronology of forts and castles is given below.

Early Times: 10,000–2000 B.C.
First prehistoric forts built on hills
Fortified towns with stone walls, such as the city of Jericho, built about 7000 B.C.
African fortifications made from stone, earth, and logs

Ancient World to 500 B.C.
People in Mesopotamia build walled cities
The Assyrians use battering rams and siege towers to attack cities like Lachish
Cities of Mycenae and Tiryns built
First hill forts

Ancient World from 500 B.C. to A.D. 500
Invention of siege catapults (about 350 B.C.)
Greeks strengthen city walls by building towers projecting in front of them
Celts of Europe build large hill forts
Romans build marching camps, legionary forts, and Hadrian's Wall
The Great Wall of China built

The Middle Ages: A.D. 500–1500
Byzantine Empire, successor to the Eastern Roman Empire, develops castle-building and siege tactics
Arabs build castles in the Middle East and North Africa
Vikings and Saxons build fortified towns
Normans develop motte and bailey castles
The Crusades: massive new ring castles are built in the Middle East and Europe
Great castles built in Wales
Cannons first used, in 14th century
Many hilltop castles and walled towns in India built
Moorish alcazars build in Spain
Walls of the city of Great Zimbabwe, Africa, constructed in 14th century
The Incas build massive stone fortresses in South America from about 1350

The Age of Cannons: 1500–1800
Renaissance engineers design low, thick-walled castles better able to resist cannon fire
Coastal gun forts and towers built
The Vauban fortress is developed
Europeans build forts in Africa, India, and North America
Great age of Japanese castles, 1560–1615

The siege of Acre of 1189. The Crusaders had the city completely surrounded, but were unable to capture it. Here an unsuccessful attempt is being made to storm the walls from the sea using siege towers rowed on galleys. On the land side, the Crusaders have constructed defenses around their own position to guard against surprise attack—both from the soldiers in the city, and from the Saracens camped in the distance.

Concrete and Steel: 1800–1945

Civil War forts, such as Sumter, built

Frontier forts built in the West

Frontier "walls," lines of gun fortresses, are built to protect Belgium and France

World War I (1914–18): trench warfare, battles for Verdun, tanks and airplanes are first used in war

World War II (1939–45): Defenses such as the Maginot Line fail to halt mobile armies supported by airpower

Modern World: 1945 to the present

Bunkers built deep underground to withstand atomic bombs

Vietnamese use tunnels as underground factories during Vietnam War

Development of tanks, airplanes, and guided missiles render old-style fortifications useless

Castles become tourist attractions, museums, or private homes

Glossary

bailey: courtyard or ward inside a castle

barbican: outer gateway protecting the main gate of a tower, castle, or bridge

bastion: a defensive position, specifically a tower open at the rear and built out in front of the main wall—often arrowhead-shaped or five-sided

citadel: a fortified palace

keep: tower stronghold within a medieval castle; called a donjon in French

machicolations: holes in gallery built out from top of wall

mantlet: movable shield used by archers

motte: mound of earth

murder holes: holes in ceiling of passage or gateway through which defenders can drop missiles on the enemy

portcullis: iron grille lowered to block a castle entrance

postern: gateway or tunnel leading out of a castle, used for surprise attacks or sallies

rampart: fortified embankment with a parapet (a low wall) on top

ravelin/redoubt: small defensive work, like a squat tower, sometimes built outside the main wall

ward: another name for the bailey or courtyard of a castle

Quotations

The Assyrian campaigns are described in the Old Testament of the Bible, in II Kings, chapters 18–20, and Isaiah, chapters 36, 37, and 39. King Sennacherib's conquests were recorded in *The Annals of Sennacherib*. The *Anglo-Saxon Chronicle* is a history of England from the time of Christ to 1154, written by monks. Shakespeare's play *Henry V* is about the English king's wars in France. The quote by Vauban comes from his book on fortifications, called *Attack and Defence* (1705–6). The sergeant who watched the attack on Fort Sumter was one of many who wrote about their Civil War experiences in diaries or letters.

INDEX